The Split Personality of a Young Girl | Mel by Day... Melanie by Night

Melek Cella

An Bright Pen-Book

Cover design by James Fitt
Cover image courtesy of
Francesco Cura | Dreamstime.com

British Library Cataloguing Publication Data.
A catalogue record for this book is available from the British Library

ISBN 978-0-7552-1381-8

Authors OnLine Ltd
19 The Cinques
Gamlingay, Sandy
Bedfordshire SG19 3NU
England

Visit us online at www.authorsonline.co.uk

Contents

Yes I am! (wait for it...)

An autobiographical piece created by one character, two identities to bring you the crazy woman behind the mask and her survival tools to her addictions...

Some days I feel very disabled, other days I feel I can conquer the world... so to speak.

I usually tend to hit rock –bottom when I pick up my pencil and note book. These two gems never leave my side where ever I go or whatever I am doing...be it the kitchen, be it the laundry room...I cook with my pencil in my hand if I have to...this is just me, when I go into the lonely zone. Mostly the best writing comes through when I am bed ridden for a few days...the pencil gets to work whilst tears let go of my painful body. Tears are the emotion and the soul of my work that will be presented here.

Are you ready to meet Mel?

Mel by Day...

Mel by Day is a collection of journal entries followed by some of my day dreams...half I lived & half I desired...

Confusion! Illusion!

I was trembling... How hard could this be?
My legs had lost their will to carry me into the room.

"Bastard!" As I mumble the very word I never thought I would repeat again, I force myself to walk in.

"I am doing the right thing here?" I say, trying to convince myself.

I jumped out of my skin as I felt a female figure rested her hand rest on my shoulder.

"H-hi..." I stutter meekly as I look up, surprised to see another ordinary woman, like myself...
"Mrs. Davis?" They asked briefly in confirmation of my identity.

Should I be talking to her?
Should I be putting my hopes up that she could possibly be the key to my freedom?

Trembling I answer "Y-es!"

This ordinary female, tall and slender, has probably never dealt with this kind of situation before. But then again, this

8

type of life experience would not have been in her job description.

"You're trembling? It's ok, you have come to the right place!", the young lady reassures me in a soft voice as she sits herself down next to me.
"I just need to ask you a few questions and then if necessary, we can take you to the women's refuge."

"Do you own half of your property?"
"Yes"
"I need his details so we can contact him"
"Why?"
"Well, he can't get away with this, look at the state of you!"
I was trembling even more so but out of fear.
"We need a contact number so we can contact him, Mrs. Davis"
"Please! I need to go and think about this long and hard before I do something stupid"
Shaking in horror in disbelief of what she was about to do.
Under her breath she started to mumble whether she would ever have the courage to...
After what seemed a never-ending walk down the long dark streets, dreading what was at stake here, I finally got home, looked at the coffee table and there were two mugs of tea accompanied by chocolate cakes...he had no idea where I had just been.

The Brain Tumour

Even if an illness is not malignant it does not mean that it does not come with long-term suffering.

It is difficult to bring up a young family after having a brain operation wipe your past from memory. I continued the struggle for many years, until one day, I decided to leap out from my comfort zone and face the world that I once knew.

I tried to take control of my own ill health and tried to improve my life, against the regular MRI scans that unfortunately revealed a slow growth tumour.

They told me that it could come back within ten years and to go and enjoy myself, but strongly warned me to make sure that I never fell or hit my head!

They had no idea that I was going back home to a five and seven year old who still needs their mum.

Me and My Path!

I always wondered what I would be like when I grew up. Never in million years did I ever think that I would be sitting here and trying to make sense of what my Brain Tumour has done to my family let alone me!

I rattled my brain (what's left of it, of course with a smile) how I am going to put this story down for me to understand what the brain tumour has done to my family. It had taken away their Mother and wife for many years.

This writing is also for my family to understand that sometimes I forget I am disabled and get carried away pushing myself out of my comfort zone. Yes, this does make me very sick to the stage that I become bed ridden to the stage where I no longer function mentally or physically for day or two. I promise I don't do it on purpose, I just simply forget when I am having fun doing what I enjoy.

My Writing!

Bloody Headaches!!

They really don't waste their time (headaches that is). As-soon as you're tired or simply drained it takes over! Or simply sad over an issue that is out of my control... and no! It is not as bad as migraine...nor is it the headache that comes with flu...

It's like you want to scream and hit your head on something...anything! And usually it takes whole lot of strong pills any pills and quietness but not darkness...a happier place with no conflict and a good 12 hours or overnight for it to go!

Basically...it wants silence... ☹

It's late in the Day

Time 22.30...headaches had overlapped to the second day continuing its poisoned claws within my head! Headaches had got worse during the day but good old nurofen and Paracetemol two of each always at hand.

Whenever I am in this state, after sleeping it off for most of the day (which is soon as the boys had left the house I hit the sack and grabbed couple of hours sleep). It's the evening... boys had gone without home-cooked food again! I have slipped out of house-wife material awhile now but at least I use to keep the home cooked food most week ends...

Now that's going out of the window too! And this saddens me, given them a reason to resent me one day if they don't already do so... My son turn to TV with silence and my husband chose to go to bed as usual. With the guilt tattooing its print on my shoulders, I turn back to my writing and for some reason I sense the outcome of all this.

How I Miss Feeling Normal ☺

14ᵗʰ of November 2011 –Sunday evening...How I long for a glimpse of normality in my life, I feel a lot better tonight. Tonight I have no numbness, no sickness, no headache, don't feel tired. As in those feelings that I am haunted with don't matter anymore...just normal tiredness. When I feel as normal as this I tend to feel ashamed of myself for opening up to you guys. World that no one seems to understand just yet (my blog... that is), but I also know that it is not here to stay (the normal feeling).

So even if I choose to delete the blog out of feeling shame, I know come tomorrow I will be back in needing space to be on my own again, back in needing to be understood because I can't make the dinner again or clean the house in quick enough time instead, I would take all day to do it! Back in needing to be understood that I can't make an effort to doll myself up to socialise whenever I am asked out I always end-up saying no.

But tonight I can do all of these things, and I honestly don't know how many hours or days it's going to last for. No, I didn't mention weeks because it never had lasted as long as a whole week before. If I am lucky, It lasts as long as two to three days the most and that is stretching it...of course not forgetting day rest about lunch time is vital...(day rest as in sleeping for few hours each day) if I was to continue this normal behaviour back in to my life, that is! And if I don't get the rest I need, I end up suffering later in the week.

Well, today I have cooked Sunday dinner and I have done all my washing and I have done some course work. I also spent time with the boys watching TV, and yes...they were in a good mood too. I guess the- boys not being in a good mood is all down to me, and how this disability controls my mood and behaviour. How it takes over my body and mind whenever it wishes to.

But now I am tired but it was bloody worth every minute of feeling normal! Yeah... when I feel good I don't stop! I couldn't... I feel as if I will never feel that feeling again so therefore I push myself...This is where I push myself out of my-comfort-zone-instead of taking it easy. I so don't believe in wasting good feelings and good mood on doing nothing.

Pushing It!

16th of November after midnight Tuesday morning time now 00.29am I swear when I started writing this post it was Monday night time 22.22pm but as slow as I am it is now after midnight heading to Tuesday morning, and I am so tired already God help me with tomorrows podcast... I am so not ready ...!

Today, more like Monday morning I was late for College, I went to bed at 03.30am. Busy writing my memoir I really wanted this memoir to be published by end of this year, if I can help it! When I set my mind on something I tend to go for it regardless of what's at stake until it's done. Yeah... I do live bit like that... like there is no tomorrow. It seems that's the only way I can get anything done.

Anyway... as I was saying... I was late going college this morning and I didn't get to do my hair or wear any make-up! That is so not like me. People, who know me, know that I am so particular about the way I look...even when they shaved my hair with the second operation; I ended up hiding my bald-head by putting my cap on to hide the baldness! Before I started this blog I use to be embarrassed about being that way, I'm sure there is a word for people like me... but not quite sure what it is... so I simply call it vain for now. Although I haven't been buying new clothes in this recession, which is so unlike me, I love to look good but I expect when the face is done and the hair looks fairly stylish it shouldn't be a problem in feeling good.

But even that is suffering at the moment because I have given 110 % to my writing and everybody who lives with me knows and probably resents me for it. They know I can only do one thing until it is done and dusted then I go on to the next thing. That's the footprints of the tumour for you! You are switched to survival mode...whatever that may be...It really depends on the individual; mine is doing what makes me happy with the career aspect, to have a career before anything else happens.

Well I can dream, can't I...?

Hard Work Pays Dividends...

22nd of November 2010. For the past three days I have only left this chair to sleep and to take my pills...as soon as I got the ball rolling with my submission to a literary agency, something snapped inside me! Adrenaline kicked in, I got the ball rolling I could not even leave the site of my lap-top so I could make tea or Turkish coffee at that matter...the only time I got to the kitchen for any of my...let say 'addictions' was after 2 in the morning and this was for the last three days....I would have said (I am not proud of doing this) but the funny thing is I AM! Because it felt bloody marvellous...To do exactly what makes you happy...is it a selfish act??? Who knows?

I am so determined that this is it! I shall carry on like this as it is... push myself to the point that I can do almost anything!
Today we had presentation day but to bring my work to the point it was...which is still not quite ready yet. There are still things that I missed out on.

As I finish today off, after cooking and feeding the boys, (Oh...of course). Mustafa couldn't hold his concern any longer – every time I push myself to this extend – that I can no longer carry on, I imagine this hurts him more than it hurts me. I don't know how to explain this to him or anyone who assumes they know me because they have been around me – but the cold truth is – I have moved to a different level – and no longer are at the place to be content with normal life anymore!

Unless I see results I am miserable – that is the truth of my little world!

Days When I Feel Like a Tramp

Tramp...In my case...most days really...24th of November Tuesday time12:28pm.

I went in late again...I can't seem to discipline my timing with my uni classes...basically I am finding it really difficult to get up anymore. Although one of the days in this week I woke up with my alarm at 6 am. I don't really know what was the cause of that... I kept my self very organised on that day, or rather morning.

I am still in search of why I am organised some days and all over the place other days. When I end-up waking up late...after grabbing hold of my mob...checking what day and time it is ...yeah...I did say day! That's because I never know what day it is - the state I wake up in, until I check with my phone to find out what's going on...what am I suppose to be doing today!

Then it hits ME!!! That's when I start panicking on days that I wake up late...I simply jump out of bed stumble all the way to the bathroom and look in the mirror...yeah, vanity don't die!...Anyway after staring at the mirror...knowing I have to ignore or deny to myself how important to my self esteem it is to look good, I completely ignore the fact that a kitchen-mop looks better then my hair...Grabbing the face wipes ...at least I can have a clean face...after I realise what day it is and start to bring my time management skills out to check... well, can I afford to put the kettle on...No! Then I have to take my pills to uni with me...out comes the carrier-bag...in goes all the pills. Next! What else, right! Put some clothes on...might help...seeing as there is no time for a shower...it is impossible to have a shower as soon as I wake up due to no balance for at least half an hour on a good day. I would probably fall and hurt myself and end –up not going in at all...all because I chose to have a shower and had an accident in it.

So, then, holding the staircase sides as I am coming down so as not to fall...I walk straight to my pills then a carrier bag then grab my books then grab the keys! In to the car and still wondering asking myself....

'woman if you are so in capable of having shower, then how the hell do you trust in driving yourself to the UNI'??? ' Then I just simply drive off...answering my own question as; people that have hope, people that have vision, people that have passion...don't just lie in bed saying Oh...I woke up late...I just skip it today...call in sick! No, they put their selves out there some times...face not washed...teeth not brushed and sometimes yeah....looking right tramp all because...they prioritise what is important!... In a disabled person's life, not their comfort...it's what their purpose is whilst they are still alive...

By the way...when I finally got to uni... time to take my pills... O...man......there were NO PILLS!!! ....to take! My medication was not with me...Panic!!! Now that never happened before!

Mix Feelings

24th of Nov! I usually don't get this quite that I have nothing to say...Usually I can still speak however sad or tired I feel-but...tonight I am speechless. Last night...rather this morning at 2 am I had a seizure...while I was typing away my assignment, but just carried on typing regardless that the leg was dead within 15 minutes, the mind must have got confused as well. Because I stood there emailing work at 2 in the morning with a dead leg. Not that I cared...I didn't! Maybe I should have...Because, after coming home however hyper I was I ended with another fit! Now that is unusual...that I don't usually have two fits within 24 hours.

Although, the idea of this page was to look back at each day, to try and understand the core of this blog and why it's up and running!
Last night, I honestly thought I was doing really well with my coursework. With each teacher with each assignment, but looking at the last assignment I delivered...I was just going through it and with a half a smile seeing...that half the key-points are still missing from it!
Now that I no longer have to do it...I see what I'm supposed to add in to it....but I am not going to cry over spilled milk. Not now...

Today I actually felt my difference regard to my hyper active character...I felt how different I was from the rest of the class....I noticed that...Because I was asking the most stupid questions and kept butting in while the teacher was talking...couldn't stop myself..Somehow as if...I was possessed by this childlike...Spoilt little girl that didn't know what to do with herself....I hate her...I hate her taking over...Luckily; she is not around for long!

However much I will try to deliver good assignments even edited by professional indexer...I will always have key-points missing and I will always have spelling mistakes in my work after it comes back from the editor. All because...I will always add some more paragraphs and that paragraph or two or three...always will stick out like a sore thumb and will be with spelling mistakes and sentence mistakes.

Never mind, it's all gone now the day is over now. Well outside is over now.

When I got home today I knew from the conversation that took place in the class that I will never be able to write professionally. I honestly thought my writing skills might improve by the third year but I guess... I was mistaken. I should take of the curtains of my eyes and see my writing for what it is and not what I dream it to be!

'Needs & Desires!'

Monday 3rd January 2011. University starts tomorrow...Am I ready to go back? No! Am I going back? God knows what I'll wake up to. Will I be going on a job hunt?

Yes! That I can tell you for sure.

But what I do know is that alarm is on for 6 am and I shall go for a jog for at least 10 minutes...well it's a start, before I make any decision...because when this decision is made it will break many people's trust in me. But...like this blog, this- is about me so it will be my choice.

1- Resolutions for New Year-no more repeated 'sorry' word
2- No more carrying guilt with me whatever the circumstances.
3- Last but not least I'll be making sure I do something every day that brings warmth to my cold heart.

Tiredness Won't Leave My Side Today...

Sunday 30th January 2011...

I have rested for the last three days but it doesn't seem to be enough. Somehow, I seem to need an extra few days this time round.

I can see it now...I can taste it now...finally the end of the course is here, the time has come to have the degree in my hand...only a few units left until I pass a Higher Education in writing, the only field I know how to throw myself in to wholeheartedly...without losing who I am! Better still, it is the only thing that I threw myself at that helped me discover who I really am.

Today I seem to feel the reasoning behind why I have been pushing myself for so long and jumping over obstacles to see the other side.

This Is What I Call News!!

12th of April 2011 time 9.45am

The consultant Reese had finally given me the all clear after 18 years of waiting for another tumour to grow!

Although I am left with limited abilities a short spun of normality almost squeezing out of me every now & again...he said "must come back if there is any suspicion of IT coming back." But as far as I'm concerned...ITS OVER!!!!

Now I have to work on how to be normal again! Maybe after I finish my studies...another two years or so..oh, and not forgetting the books...then I'll consider looking after the unfit body that had been screaming for movement but enable to deliver.

Not Knowing What You're Going To Wake Up To...

After midnight, 13th of December!
Where does time fly...?

I have once again found myself on the cross roads in my life.
This time it hit me harder but saying that I think as I get
older I seem to care less and less. Nothing seems to matter
except what is happening for that present day, for that hour,
for that minute, for that second... nothing seems to matter
when you are hurt...

Then you wake up, Pulse with a life of its own pumping...
Need to breathe, need to live!
That's when you realise you have to be strong.

Joy Ride!

I was asked to take the grandchildren to school in the morning

Pick them up in the afternoon

Wake up six o'clock in the morning to take my morning pills

So I become a responsible adult!

Hmm...

Then straight to the kids ...deliver them to their destination...

Now pull over time for a fag...

Back on a motorway

...oh, this feels good...

The morning drive with no traffic

...foot down oh...

Baby this feels so good!

I almost enjoy delivering the kids to their destinations...

Ok I behave myself...

What I meant to say was I enjoy having the responsibility of the school run from seven in the morning up until half seven. Although the traffic builds up by afternoon collection...I still make the most of driving. I don't honestly know who benefits here more my daughter for having the girls out from under her feet so she can go to work or the kids...That they are with someone who cares for them or me...Me!! The crazy me...

College Years!!

When I first started uni, I didn't know what hit me. The elegancy, mixture of superiority and if that's not enough hot...hot teachers...mentally and physically in your face.

After the first few months I put this front on as if I knew what I was doing and kept a straight face most of the time. I swear they must have thought I was a mental case, now they know...I definitely am! I would get them to repeat their words every few sentences. They must have thought I am lying to them.

It took me over six months to open up and tell the teachers the truth. The truth about my learning difficulties, that's the reason I have to get them to repeat their sentences. Not forgetting I badly stair when I am tired so who knows what they thought of that. Mental case, I presume...

But yet, they didn't give up on me, even when I gave up on myself. Each month I would honestly give up studying the course. But one of my teachers he seemed really difficult to understand. Bad enough there was a language barrier, but this was huge...for me anyway. It was more like an accent barrier, for that I hated being on the course for the first half of the year so much. It was basically about how we would have a lecturer in the class then I would go home to open up my note book to nothingness. Absolutely brain dead! What was I to do? So after picking on main teacher for not getting his lecturing...I stopped and instead try to tell them that I have disability in learning, and am very slow at grasping things.

That must have shocked the hell out of them all. Saying all, I had three teachers in one year and four teachers in the second year. Not one of them understood the way I spoke, even the one that saw potential in me. He is everyone's mentor including mine. Every child that passed through his teaching path has come through to be something marvellous.

He insisted, with the questions I threw in between his lecturing...I say I threw only because I had found it hard at the first year to act like a student and put my hand up and wait so I had this tendency to throw words in the middle of lecturing and expected him to respond to my question to simplify the subject. Yeah...I really was this difficult.

But, yet he persevered...the more questions come out of my mouth the more answers come out of his mouth. Within a few months I started to enjoy his class and him. He is definitely an icon of the course. Although he isn't the main teacher who started the whole writing course I believe the course would not be what it is without him.

Saying all of that about one teacher, they all had something special about themselves.

The main teacher who started the actual course has a way of pushing, guiding, supporting all of his students to the best of their abilities. Without him the course would have not existed. So a lot of the achievements of his pupils come from him steering in the back ground.

My first class were in their twenties. Lovely bunch, miss them so much. Very clever bunch!!

But my second class that I stayed back to finish the two year course in three years pushed me into the next class that came after me. They were very different characters altogether. I didn't even socialise with these characters in my personal time.

In my third year I decided to keep away from everyone. It wasn't that hard to keep away from the new class seen as they made it clear that they didn't have time for me. How do I know this? I know it from them refusing to give me their emails or fb names when I asked so we can be friends. Since then I just focused on getting a best seller out one-day...so here I am...and probably the only thing that I sleep and wake up to. No...I don't hate people; I just need space to re-charge my batteries to be able to live normal life now and again. This recharging takes place mostly once a day, two to four hour sleep or I would suffer huge consequences out of mental exhaustion. So there...that's why I say to people that Their Husbands are safe with me. I will not steal them...in fact I'm looking for someone to give my husband to. Any takers...??

Leaving the joke aside, I have come through all of that long three year course and to be honest I don't know who is more proud of me...My teachers for actually making it this far...or me for achieving something I never thought it was possible!!

My First Assignment

In 2008, I signed onto this course. You know those courses that are just a short course that teach you things or refresh your memory with a certificate at the end of it. After a short while of starting I was sent these forms to fill in, what do I know...so then I showed it to my daughter. You guys should have seen her face. It was a picture! She lifted her head up from the forms and said mum...do you know what you have signed onto?? Errmm...a writing course. Mum...This is like what I just finished a Higher Education Degree. My god mum...You are going to uni...This is university that you are signing onto. I think it's great! Mum I am so excited for you; my mum is going university...Wow!! She gave me a huge cuddle and a big smile. But I still didn't know what revolved around Higher Education. I just took her words for it until she filled-up the forms for in me.

Within weeks we were asked to submit an assignment in called "Hot Face" It was all about dead people and a funeral parlour. I thought I did a good job even though I got a referral for it...I didn't pass my first assignment. Now that I have finished the course I am looking back onto all of the referral assignments and laughing at myself at how bad my understanding of an essay was. About three long paragraphs put together makes an assignment. Not forgetting that I've never been to school. But I swear my teacher did say to me...He isn't looking for academic ability...this course isn't academic course it is purely creative-a measure of one's ability to create original work. Oops...well, I am f# #ked then!

Since then I had been terrified to deliver work to the teachers. It felt like I was submitting my recipes to magazines...knowing full well that within two weeks there will be an envelope with a rejection letter in it. If anything scared the hell out of me out of the three years of education would be the assignments!! Ohh...was chilling!

Depression at its Element ☹

Morning of 6th of June 2011

Wed... alarm goes off at 6.00am

I pull the quilt upwards snuggling under it

Then it hits me

Grandchildren!!

Out of bed...

Have 15 minutes to get in the car...Damn

Tea and pill's have to wait until I finish the school run

Same trousers go on, same top goes on

Into the car

Reverse

Damn it...feel so numb...just hope the roads are clear, just in case, in any case...

School run is over

As I drop the last kid off to school, I pull out a fag and light it...

I savour it by watching the building construction builders already a few hours into their work by now. I have been at it since 6. Boy, roads are so good to drive on that early in the morning or very late at night. Peaceful isn't the word. Although I am still half asleep, I do look forward to being on the road.

Now I am exhausted. Today somehow the energy is next to nothing. I feel it. It feels like I've been on drugs last night and the after effects have lingered on. Or like when you have too many to drink, we are talking about first thing in the morning thought. In my case I don't have to do any of them, I am drunk from exhaustion...period!!! Maybe I stay with just writing one piece today and get some rest seen as I have to be alert for them later on. Boy-I-do-feel-f##k#d ☹

A collection of poetry and short stories
exploring the various personalities of
Melanie Cox

Melanie by Night...

Melanie has linked her poems and short stories with Mel's day-to-day journey by bringing you original and unique work.

Devil Awakes Within the Night

His muscling claws digging into blood thirsty thighs
Sweat accumulating from fear mixed into pleasure

She can no longer push him away
She fears him like never before
She tastes the devil's desire for her soul

It is so tangible
That you could mistake her for the devil
And him for the innocence of just following his orders by the
higher source

She takes his claw and presses it to her breast
Felt an enormous pleasure having the upper hand over the
devil himself
To dominate the devil into her pleasure she never thought she
had it in her.

Nothing Is Set In Stone...

One isn't born with successes or a dream
One isn't born bored nor enthusiastic
One isn't born to know what's waiting for them around the
corner!
What one is born with is hunger for mummy's love and
breast
Cuddles that wrap you around their chest
Soft hands that gently caress your cheek,
Carefully not wanting to hurt you, delicate thing

We do forget how precious these moments have been
Now that we are holding our own bundle,
We no longer need their old freckly hands that feel like
Sand paper to the touch

We no longer have time for them or need their time
The only time we miss them is when they are no longer here.

I Am Alive

When all the lights turn off
When all the noise shuts off
By human hand
The expectations die down with the darkness
It leaves me alone with hope.

My mind goes crazy
Wondering if
I have taken anything out to defrost
For tomorrows cooking
If everyone's clothes are ironed
If I left everyone happy before they hit the sack.

I quietly climb downstairs
Switch on my computer
Get my home work out

I say to myself it will be ok when you finish this course
There will be another light out there waiting for you.
Then I suddenly feel alive once again

Temptation!

I know I've been this way before
Whenever I find myself infatuated with
life
Everything it has to offer
I want to be one with nature

Beauty grabs my mind
With its devilish playful style
Blinds me with desire
With its inescapable pleasure.

I find myself escaping from the truth
Running away from myself
Hope to be captured by it
Not caring of the consequences.
Tasting the paradise...

Fantasy

Another day over
Stretching my tired aching limbs
Gagging for a hot shower
To massage every aching inch of my body

Buttons...

One-by-One

Undone!

Silk blouse
Cresses my tired skin as it falls
Stepping into the steaming hot shower
While it works itself through
The heat envelopes me from within

Tenderly teasing
Each and every limb
And muscle
Defusing the tension of daily stress
Caused by sitting in front of the desk

Reminding me of my needs and the neglect
Screaming in a high pitched tone!

Why?

Why neglect me?

And once again
I let it take over
Surrendering to its foreplay
Each drop
Turning into thousand beads
Crushing onto yesterday's pain.

Leaving The Past Behind ☹

Fingers won't hold as well as they should
Limps let go the site of their duties
Eyes have lost their site
Ears won't let the world in
Something has changed
The machine once was there for me
Now...no longer exist

Reprogramming
Taking on the work of neurologist
Is it the God given work?
Or is it our sheer hard work
Bloodshed and sweat
The challenges
That we put our disabled bodies through
Must be the case
That brings our bodies back to life

Post – Operation ☹

Post-Operation
Feeling sick this morning
Woke up with dizziness & light headedness
Due to eight hour anaesthetic
Shouldn't expect anything less

Want to throw-up but there is nothing there
Want silence
But the noise of the patients in pain
Is deafening
Want to close my eyes
But the observation nurse won't let me

Burning eye lids
Dry peeling cheeks
Itchy sour head

Wrapped-up
In a bandage
Ready to be signed...
(An autograph please...would you?)

Can't lift the wounded head
Up to the doctor's call
But all he wants is to do his job
To make sure
That the operation
Was a success
So I won't be another patient
Suing him for the errors
Or the famous word of compensation... no doubt!

Me & My Pencil ☺

Placed my pencil on lined paper
But it won't slide on its own
I draw a silhouette of a letter A to begin with
It lost its way in the dark.

When it came to end of a sentence
It reaches the danger-zone...no left ...no right
No sign to follow
It looks back on itself
Gets dizzy staring
Staring at a...what looks like
A maze from where he is standing.

Even our pencil needs a nudge at times
To knock the fear out of them.

To cross over

Turning their nightmares
Into an emotional sentence
Paragraphs to chapters
Page by page...

Yes my friend without you
I will not exist!

1st Of March 2011!!

I met someone
Who changed my life
Turned my head around
Changed my outlook
And
Threw the depression
Out of site!

I met someone who changed my life
The strength...I become...
Following the footsteps one-by-one
I met someone who changed my life
Started to see my life through
Love, Passion, joy and learned what being happy is about

I met ME!!
Without me
Nothing would be worth living!

Le Femme

Quality of hair
Keep it short
Keep it long
Wear it to match
Make-ups & nail crafts

Hair is usually the canvas of a girls look
It is what gives her the confidence
To hold what is hers

High hills
Low hills
Trainers & flip flops
Knee highs & ankle boots
Girl's best friend
...is their 'Looks'

Miniskirts to fancy dresses
Natural lips
To red hot pouts

Their power
Is in their looks
They own the floor and pull the goods

Blue attentive warm eyes
Green glittering cat eyes
Black seductive sex eyes
All is hidden behind girl's power!

Key to access
Key to success
It's our feminism & charm
That men can't live without!!

Childhood

I'm like a bird... can't be caged-up
But yet
Married as soon as I hit puberty!
I have an eye to live an out-law life
But yet
Have a routine family life
Feel suffocated in a crowd
But yet
Have people around for dinner
I wasn't brought up...I grew-up
Not in family surroundings
But war and poverty!

Never knew what it's like to hear my name to be called out
For breakfast
For dinner
Or simply doing wrong as a child
But yet
Tasted the coldness of an empty kitchen when hungry
Empty rooms when I needed cuddles.
The only thing that made us a family
Was the DNA that we carried.

Celebration of War

Drums are hitting hard
Tanks are walking by
Roads shattering
Noises are overlapping each other
Is it joy —is it war —
or is it figment of your imagination - of what one needs and
desires - to take their selves away from the reality

Not every drum noise is a joy
Not every tank means a war
Celebration is given mix feelings to those that left standing
Not every child is hopeful
Not every teacher is ready to teach the once left behind
The anguish the pain the joy – how do you explain to a kid
where his house is
The door they walked out of this morning will not belong to
them in the evening
How do you explain to a child that your enemy is simply
doing its job as a soldier?
Never met you – you are just a flesh – and his job is to stop
your pulse beating
How do you differentiate animals from mankind! When all
along we end each other lives
How do you???

Pre – Celebrations

Feeling safe were never an option –
Fear was like a second skin
Then there were adults who never did get any sleep
Fear simply haunted them –

Waiting for that drill to kick-start
So they can grab the first weapon they can reach
Waiting for the sirens
Looking out for the tanks
Safety was never an option

You somehow knew war was only lurking around corner
That's just how adults felt
What about my generation – I was only seven
Was it all a game to us kids?
Was it all an adventure to 7-8- year olds?
Was it a night mare waiting to happen?
To engrave in our hearts
And we were only kids

....

It didn't matter what age you were
It didn't matter what nation you were

What mattered was – that you stayed faithful to one side
and one side only

It didn't matter that you wake up every morning looking at
a
Soldier
Guarding
It didn't matter
But on face value - people acted normal
This was no war – There are no enemies

Man from both nations would sit at the cafe having coffee
Playing backgammon –
While the big guys
Planned our death

When all along

People
Ordinary people just like you and me - want to get along
But!!! - That didn't matter
Nothing mattered

BIG GUYS were out there to kill

Bath-Time

Looking through the window
December snow blanketed over the fields
Christmas decorations
Bring warmth to my cold heart
As the tub filled my bath with bubble bath
The dressing gown slides off.

Naked shoulders
Facing the bathroom window

Music goes on!

He goes off..

...and I go high!

Toes teasing the water
Stepping into an inviting tub
Breathing the aromas
Mixture of vanilla
Rose
&
Lily cuddles

On my steamed window ledge
Keeping it warm
While the snow from outside keeping it cool.

A bit like yin and yang

Sinking slowly into a million bubbles...
The silky feeling caressing the wounded
Taking the moment to reflect
On what might have been.

I push myself up upwards
To change the music
To something more romantic
As I stand up
Bubble baths are having a field day on my pair...
Dancing away to the music
Drew a heart on steamed glass
Inches away from the outside world
Still shining what looked like a glittered dress
Getting ready for her Christmas party
Not everyone was alone
Even my window had someone, or something to shine for.

Lying back in the bath-tub

Surrendering to its tease
Closed my eyes to the music
To my window
Most of all...to my pain.

Sun Dominates with Kindness

Sunlight hitting my window

In the middle of a summer mist

I stir and pull my cover over my head

I've-got so much to write

So little time!

Then there is the BA (Hons) to worry about.

The emptiness of the room

The emptiness of my heart

But hold-on a minute...what emptiness?

I spend three years or so developing my thoughts and ideas

I spend another three years before that building up my name

The legacy of it!

Surely out of those six years I held onto something or another...

Then comes off the bed-cover turning towards the blinds...

The blinding sunshine

Out I get out of my cocoon of a bed

Out comes the pencil

My right arm

My saviour!

Coffee V Tea

Step outside of my skin

Or

Rather my backdoor

Took my strong black coffee

Accompanied with large mug of very hot tea

Sit on the steps closing the door behind me.

For a smoker this is ridiculous that I hate the smell of fags

It lives lingering a stale smell...

And

Inhale...bliss

Watching magpie

Stretching his wings flying up in the sky

Salute and smile

I fear for all the wrong it brings

I fear for all the right it might bring.

But here I am

Tea then coffee

Gratefully

Finds its way

Where is most lonely.

Inhaling poison

Poison that relaxes and numbs

Poison that you no longer give a dumb.

The nerves

Is letting go of my limbs

Letting go of my mind

The world becomes more apparent

Break-Time

Towel softly settles over a freshly cut grass

The gown gently slides off my pure white flesh

Exposing the two inch bikini barely covering

Coconut tan lotion feels greasy, sticky and sweaty

But aching for his hands

To play the part

Laying on my towel imagining

Imagining rubbing his hands up and down

Gently rubbing his hands... I then turn around to face him

His face looks serious...his chest has developed film of shine from sweat

I take his oily hands pushing him under my bikini...teasing him...or rather me self...

I then turn around and take his manhood into my wet hot and oily palms

Putting the fingers to work...he doesn't waste time

I gasp...

By now sweat pearls on my sun heated breast... or is it him that is causing this heat...

I am burning with desire

The more he moves his fingers

The more I stir

Neighbours out in the garden

I can hear the gossip

The fence is law, I can see their faces

But who cares

From the stir he creates within me

I take him into my mouth

Cock

Meets

Tongue

I gasp with a relieved tension and then he gasps and stands up to give the thumbs up to the neighbours saying...

"You right mate!!"

Uncertainty

War

Guns and Rifles

Illegal invasions

Sex and Drugs

Gun handed into child's little hands

Which ones would be more dangerous to one?

Is not clear to eye

Until you get close to taste the cold bloodshed

Children are shot

Old folks cut to pieces

Or...

Buried alive

But some still think sex and drugs are more dangerous

You still have a pulse on drugs

But...

Don't have a damn chance if you are already slaughtered...

What about tanks??

The broken roads caused by the army...

The illegal invasion surrounds us

Be it Britain

Be it America

Be it Greece

Be it Turkey

Be it Cypriot Islands

Be it all above

More that I lost count off...

War don't give a damn

However there is always hope from sex and Drugs.

Hunger!

Makes one needy

Crave most unfairly

Decent don't come to equation of norm

Stealing and killing is the only survival truth

Isn't that where the selfishness crept upon us?

Silent Thoughts

I am the river that overflows with joy

I am a rock that holds its ground

I am the army that surrounds you

I am the core of your anger your passion your outcome

I am the heart-beat of your vision

Take me now!

Embrace me forever!

Yesterday's pain is no longer here

Tomorrow may never come

But

But

No promises that you won't taste pain again

But without pain there are no pleasures so...

Embrace me because I am your best friend and worst enemy!!

Figment of Imagination

I want you now!

I want you as you stand in my mind

I want you today not tomorrow

But when you stand in front of me

Oddly

The desire becomes confused

Is it the chase that we desire and not the bait??

It's like fishing in an uninhabited river after dark

Once caught you lose your appeal

Inspiration Needs Helping Hand

I was asked "where do you get your inspiration from?

- From songs?

- From stories?

-From sea, sand, and naked bodies?

I replied...

Open your front door and wait!

The next day he said-

I open my door and waited and nothing happened.

I then said-

Did you feel the wind?

Did you listen out to the crowd?

The next day he said –

I did but still nothing happened.

I then said...

What did you expect...?

For the words to climb-up and place their-selves onto your pc?

The leg work has to come from you!

Secret Pleasures

She can smell the stale cigarette smell. It really doesn't suit her. her hair may look funky but it bloody stinks...it's that smell that puts her off of being a chain-smoker...so she only smokes every now and again, usually when she takes a journey to memory lane or when she needs to break away from her demons...

The house is empty, she needs to unwind-far too intense to concentrate on her work. Bailey's out fags out...The dildo is out...the clouds and the fog has created cosy mood within her now.

Slippers off as she stroll upstairs

T-shirts off by third steps

Zip ...undone, skirt down her ankle almost to the top

Facing the shower...imagining the hot powerful shower head working its way over her attention seeking shoulders...and as she steps in rolled down the knickers.

Then the imagination takes over...steaming millions pearls hitting onto a softly tanned skin. She Lets a sigh.

Each inch of her body has been harassed by the hot steamed shower almost burning painfully getting it ready for pleasure that waits for it. Her eyes reach to the corner of the bed...seeing her toys they are ready sitting waiting for her order....what order?? Have no control over anything when she is in her own world. Anything and everything is possible and is at hand. Shower off as it gives her his little cheeky smile...as if he knows what's at store for her.

Walks out the shower throws herself over the bed lining all wet...

Breasts-perky waiting for attention

Lotion loaded naked body

And she grabs the dildo...

Me & My Left Arm

I don't usually make friends, talk to people but don't keep them close.

I met a young lady who looks everything that I am not. But she does insist that we are very much alike.

She drinks-I don't

She smokes —ok I started

She goes through men like nobody's business- well, I used to until I gave myself to my writing

She is destructive- well, I am only destructive when I am with her

But...but...but...

I guess she is right we are very much alike!

We have the most fun when we are together!

We are at our highest creatively when we are together!

She calls us foreign soul-mates...

I call us two wrongs -when together never more right.

Racing With Alarm Clock...

Sudden shock

My eyes literally opened up half way out of bed

I can't hear the alarm

Million thoughts going through my head

I'm late??

I didn't hear the alarm...crap!!

I'm late??

Trying to lock my focus onto the time

Numbers are read...5.45am

Smile entered my face...

My body relaxed into cheeky mode

As if I was in a race with the alarm clock

...and I got there before it did...I won!!

Hmm...1-0 to me...

Jealousy Comes in Many Forms

I am jealous of my friend

Although, I don't mix with

I don't know where

I certainly crave for it!

Like hungry war-child craves for food,

Like thirsty war-child craves for water,

Hoping for the heart-beat...to never stop

Pulse beating at the death of gun-shots

Drugs

&

Alcohol

More than joy-ride I steal the car for

More than cuddles

More than sex

More than an orgasm

That all the above sets...

Gives me strength

Shows me the path

The desire of one's vision

Can only be found when YOU are around!

Wonder

Wonder what the world is coming to

Sitting in my seat freezing my balls

Ripped trouser and old shirt

Why would people take me seriously?

Why would people believe that I am more than my looks!

When there are well groomed idiots who take your place and add to the distraction of what's left.

World revolves around illusions that are created by delusional nut-cases

Wouldn't it be better if the prisoners where set free

Replace them with people outside, and then we'll see what the world comes to??

World of Wonders- Future Seeks

Age V Life

Tattoos & piercings

Botox & breast implants

Eye lifts & face lifts

Cosmic surgeries and here comes...

The tumour that fucks one's life UP!!

It takes four years to let you eat or recognise the taste of water...yeah, as if water has taste??

It takes five years to let you stand up properly to take your kids to school...well, by then the kids are five years older then you last set your eyes on them. So go for it!!

It takes six years to admit that you have a limp and have no balance so the kids kind of embarrassed when you limp them to school and back...and beg you to stay at home!

Then comes the moment of truth...you get so bored sitting on your ass all day that you pretended that you are better and want to work!

But, no work is available for your ability in year 1999.

Broken accent, unstable leg, blurred speech, and huge ego that you never been here before, therefore...have no idea how the hell to accept what it is that you become!!!!! Especially if your family haven't accepted it yet!!!

Well, since then, I left home many times out of depression, I got myself a part time job, I started taking my medication with firstly diet coke then light alcohol then stuck with Bailey's-nice touch! Good combination!! I then started Martial Arts...kicked some butts...no, not with the dead-leg! But still got up to Green-Belt! Come-on...Twice with the dead leg I broke a brick as well.

So, now after all the drama and in between all of that last three years I threw myself to a course...while the husband threatened to leave me...I was kind of hoping he would. But never happened! No, what has happened is I have graduated from a non-academic writing course that I attended after publishing a recipe book...Don't ask me how that happened ....Haven't got the foggiest idea!!

Now I am still alive and still kicking...and as a matter in fact thinking of getting Botox done, lipo-suction, thigh suction, stomach ...well, getting on, youthfulness don't hang around waiting for you to recuperate from ill health. ☺

Surrendering

Why is it one can never say no?

When has it become a chore?

Should it hurt a pleasure like you never tasted before?

The screams mixed with ecstasy and pain?

Bodies speak a different language to each other?

One is begging the other is not listening

Sweat glands are pouring with pleasure

Arms and legs are tensing with sorrow

One's pushing and one's pulling

How can one distinguish sex from rape!!

Oh Daddy

I'm ready for school daddy

I eat my porridge daddy

Brushed my teeth and comb my hair just the way you wanted
daddy

But after hours of waiting at the gates I no longer hear your
footsteps daddy!

The road you walked on

The places you worked at

The domineer you carried with you

Is a walking shadow left unattended?

I miss you daddy

Enduring affairs

Situations

No longer

Open for your footsteps

The deep voice

One arm hug

Reassuring eyes glittering with a twinkle

You were my shining hope to my future that's come and gone...

You left me unattended

I grew up alone

Not as your daughter but a lost soul.

Now I look back

Wandering if the dead really follow the living their every step

Were you there when I got married?

Where you there when I gave birth to your grandchildren?

Were you there when I made life changes????

Where you there...???

Are you still there with the drastic change I am about to make???????

I need you

I need your acceptance

I need you to tell me everything I chose for myself is ok with you

Because I moved on daddy

Because...I no longer need you daddy

I love you enough to let you go Daddy

After years of denying your death I finally accepted you're gone forever

May you rest in peace daddy xx

Whatever Next

Burning yearning

Crazy bitch turning

90 degrees to south

Husbands on leach

No girls safe

She can take you and me

Swallow whole

Chew and spit out

Require higher taste

Threesome

Orgies

Nude camp

Whatever you desire

For grand-dad $50 and the old-girl can watch...

If Only The World Could Speak!

Why chip on a shoulder??

The gullible says...

Colour and status should not matter

But the road rage blindly rejects

Is it me or is it you??

World is no longer here for me and you

The green grass turning blue feeling sorry for itself due to
lack of H2o

Trees are crying because humans have eaten their babies

Who says the word is here for you and me??

The animals are hiding from butchers

But due to end of the world there is neither shelter nor mercy

World is not here for me and you

It don't owe you anything

But you owe it a great deal

For fucking it up BIG TIME...!!!

Tell Him

Angelino couldn't sleep a wink all night. It was the middle of summer and very humid. Both of the windows were open. All she had on was her skimpy night dress. She turned round and looked at him lying there, looking devilishly handsome with his tan. Tom was a good looking man, he had turned heads all of his life. Even when he was a young boy he was admired for his looks.

She couldn't resist harassing him in his sleep. But tonight was different he had been working very late and was absolutely exhausted. She was feeling hot and bothered, but tired- Angelino placed her warm soft lips with gentle kisses from his neck to his toes, slowly caressing his back in this heat. Tom started to stir and turned around, probably imagining he was in a dream- like state.

She carried on leaving wet patches of her gentle lips all over him. By now, she was ready for some action.
In the morning, when Tom woke up he was so embarrassed to look at his wife's face, that he rushed out of the house without breakfast. She was left wondering.

Religion V Sex

*Hanging her cross over her bedside, she goes down
onto her knees to pray. Her every breath she takes to say
Amen, her thoughts go straight to his naked body that is
lying on the crisp white sheet. Looking across the room the
portable fan is blowing cool air over him; she finishes her
prayer with a guilty conscience and slips -in beside him -
gently runs her finger nails over his back, running her nails
from his neck down. He turns over as he stirs in his sleep, she
gets all giddy about the thought of abusing him in his sleep
so she runs her finger nails from his chest down to his toes,
by this time, turning herself on, she decides to take her
lingerie off.*

*Unaware of waking him up, she continued to seduce him.
But it wasn't him she was seducing. Sweat started to pearl
on her skin, he liked it that way. She remembered him saying
so. His body lying all relaxed spaced out. She pulls away to
position her lips gently over his chest, placing gentle kisses.
First kiss followed the second, third and so forth. Before she
knew it she was fighting herself not to take his breast into
her moist mouth. She places her breast onto his avoiding*

putting weight on him but he was stirring with a smile on his face..........

She finds herself waking up-to an alarm-clock...to her surprise she finds herself tangled into the duvet...covered in a million droplets of moisture - staring at her cross at her bed side.....

Living Coma

Mary's birthday was coming up so she invited a few of her neighbours round, she thought nothing of it. After everyone had left, she started to pick up the wine glasses and the plates, to clear up and vacuum before she had her shower.

"Why do you tease me like that?" Tom asked. His eyes couldn't stop scanning her bare legs; she was swaying one foot in front of the other as if she were on the cat-walk, modelling her legs. They were shining from where he was sitting, with six-inch heels, eye-catching red party shoes, thin stripes covered with shimmering stones, teasing sensually her sun-kissed legs, she had a golden tan. His eyes were glued to her magnetic walk, travelling upwards slowly to her shapely thighs. He could taste the coconut oil she soaked her body in after every shower. He took a deep breath; he was turning himself on and started to rub himself over his jeans, getting a hard-on now, just by watching her bare flesh - because that's what she was to him. Nevertheless he needed to do something about it.

As she bent down to pick up the empty wine glasses, he poked her ribcage with his finger. She had been drinking and was very tipsy by now and giggling but not exactly sure what his intentions were.

"I saw you flirting with Charlie all night; you're fucking him, aren't you?"

"Seeing as I can't fuck you, I've got to fuck someone," she felt like dirt, but it didn't stop her. "It's ok for you to have an itchy dick but I can't have itchy knickers, ha..!" She didn't believe her ears, what was she saying? She was too drunk to care.

"Is that so?!" His face changed.

"You don't fuck me, what you do is rape me, you piece of shit," her anger was rising out of control "and dump me aside bruised, like I'm part of the meat market, 'Fuck what you want, and dump what you don't', isn't that your policy? I'm not to sleep with other men. You bruise me so much; do you honestly think there is a man who is willing to put their neck out there to fuck me with a husband like mine, after they see my bruised body?" His mind suddenly grasped the direction her words were going in; she was digging herself into an early grave and didn't know it.

"I know why you beat me up, so I can't find another man. Congratulations! Let me tell you something, if that is why you treat me the way you do, don't bother. Lucky for me I was too clever for you. I've already had my fair share of men while you were fucking around with girls, from young to old,

I didn't sit and wait for you to fancy a bit of me all these years. In fact I've had it with you and any other man for that matter."

Tom couldn't believe his ears, what he was hearing from his innocent wife.... "You had it with other men, ha! You missed having my cock in your fucking big mouth, you missed sucking. Ha!" Half out of his pants by now, he was swaying at her. "Why don't you just come and get it? You fucking whore!" As he rubbed with his hand playfully, "I have to do that job for you as well." He caught her bare arm, Mary wouldn't have any of it, "What, one isn't enough for you?"

"Who did you fuck then? Do I know them? Not my work mates? They would laugh behind my back! You whore!" He tried to grab hold of her thigh between the split of her dress; he had to leave his mark on her. It was overdue.

"You disgust me," Mary spat, aiming at his face. "It's ok for you to fuck every woman that you see young and old, you pervert. Isn't that what you did with me, ruined a fourteen-year-old girl's life? You fucking men are all the same."

Tom could stand it no longer, listening to her making a fool of him. Swinging a back-hander to her left cheek, he watched her crash onto the floor, holding her face.

"I disgust you, you forget I am a man, it's not my fault if a slag lies under me, after I finish with them I pull my trousers back on: I'm still the same man. I'm not the one who's a whore." He watched the strength in her face, she wouldn't go down that easily. He continued, needing to break her strength. "The whores beg for it, I've actually done them a favour, scratched where their wimp husbands couldn't reach."

Mary couldn't believe her ears, all these years she'd been living with this man and didn't see who she was married to. He wasn't acting normally anymore. As she continued with clearing up, she planned how to run away from him. As she approached the kitchen sink she felt a thump on her right thigh throwing her onto the sink and leaving her in shocking pain. He tattooed her leg with his own knuckles using a ring attached to his finger: he had to have his mark on her. That's how he liked it.

"Charlie thought you looked great with your new figure, ha!" He had a weird sense of humour.

As Mary turned round, he pushed her head back, grabbing her neck, trying to strangle her, calling her a slag at the same time. By this time she was trying hard to push the hand away that was latched onto her neck. Her eye-balls showed signs of strain as she tried to shake him of her. By now she was gasping for air, trying to shake all of her body in order to loosen his hold on her. He finally took his hand off her neck and watched her helpless body fall onto the kitchen floor, so tired of what she has with him.

Tom fell onto his knees, and started to stroke her cheek tenderly, full of fear. He examined his hand mark that was dampened with tear drops, and realised he was actually looking at a very beautiful woman. When did she grow-up? He thought to himself. It wasn't too long ago that he'd asked this under-age girl to marry him. He no longer could see the supple cheeks on Mary. The mature skin on her face was soft but aged, covered by now with old make-up that was moist with warm tear drops, and her piercing blue eyes were bloodshot, terrified of crying anymore than she already had. He wanted her like he never wanted her before; he started to ask himself why he had never noticed her before. She could see this in his eyes and tried to calm him down hoping that he may just spare her life. She didn't care about anything else, not even rape. "Not anymore." She didn't care how much pain he was about to inflict on her. Finally she had made up her mind: if she survived this she would kill him herself with the first chance she got. As he started to rip her clothes off, he could see why other men were fantasising about his wife, he couldn't shut his mind off. Another blow, but this time it went straight to her stomach, he continued beating her, black and blue, poor Mary was too drunk and drained to scream for any of the neighbours to hear. She felt she was about to pass out from the pain, but he would not let her close her eyes; he wanted her to see what pain she was causing him. With one hand over her mouth, he forced himself into her, pulling her long blonde hair hard; a few strands came out in his hand. Not even her nail scratches on his pale face could stop him; he couldn't help but get pleasure as he watched himself push back and forth, digging in hard and watching her squeal in pain. Eventually she became empty bodied, lifeless, just lying there letting him get on with it. He couldn't come: he needed her to scream. Finally he hung on to her child-bearing hips with his beastly hands and would not stop until she passed out.

The nurse, running towards Tom, called out, "She's waking up, her husband is screaming in excitement."

Tom was finally going to rejoice with his bride. Tom could not hold his tears back in aged eyes that had not seen sleep for ages. Mary was slowly waking up to the fact that the nurse was making a fuss, and her husband was hovering over her, eager to kiss her. When she finally opened her eyes, she turned round to see the man who had just raped her. She let out a piercing scream at him to "leave her alone!" acting on the last thing she remembered before she fainted. When the nurses explained to her that she'd been in a coma for the last five years, she stared into the air, shocked by what she had woken up to. The tears she had held back each time he abused her turned into a river, she could not hold back another drop.

(Which-One-Are –you??)

Mel's Quotes & Sayings

- *-Government is like an abusive partner.*
- *People say trust your instincts...what happens when you're dopey most of the time...your instincts would be saying fuck you...fuck everything!*
- *In my family...I have to be on my guard...so not to take their frowns away from their faces...otherwise they would not know what to do with smiles.*
- *Ones make –up is made of 30% nature and 70% nurture. As they get older and education takes over...it wipes the context out of the window...*
- *When I was a kid I use to believe in hell and heaven...now all I believe in is... if I don't sit here to write my book...it won't write itself...Nothing happens on its own just because you're religious.*
- *Failing doesn't hurt me...but not learning from my failure does.*
- *Life is one big rape...if you let it!*
- *One's ability or talent should not lie under the letters that come after their name!*
- *There is a thin line between hard sex and rape!*
- *Hardest pain to contemplate is usually the one that we inflict upon ourselves.*
- *People would only stop from hurting us, if we stop showing them the way.*
- *When is sex counted as rape??*

- *You become the devil himself if you spend enough time with him*
- *Women enjoy hard sex as long as it doesn't hurt them!*
- *One day I dream of making love to someone sexually attractive!*
- *Girl only has one man in her life that she can trust and is not necessarily her daddy in this case or her brothers.*
- *When something or someone is available, one no longer has the desire for them.*

www.ingramcontent.com/pod-product-compliance
Lightning Source LLC
Chambersburg PA
CBHW060427290526
45791CB00002B/887